Inheritance

Jason Weis

BookLeaf
Publishing

India | USA | UK

Presentation by *BookLeaf Publishing*

Web: www.bookleafpub.com

E-mail: info@bookleafpub.com

ISBN: 9789358317787

First edition 2024

*For everyone I could and couldn't write a poem
for — thank you for filling my life with joy*

Of Sweet Things

Only a taste at first, soon thirst
Our mouths agape, a shared device
Only something so sweet

Would suffice

Wrapped around your finger
Whisper in my ear
Wound about and bound to you

My dear

Might you be that one
Missing for so long
Make me believe again

In song

I thought I caught the tune
Inflected by the throat of time
Inspiring all who heard

Our rhyme

Only something so sweet

Our song alone to share
Only a taste at first

Skill Issues

It was never a matter of chance
She said
She'd leave us at a time to be decided
A candid moment always showing
What she'd left for dead

Only one possessed as she
Of loss
Could speak as such of love beyond her
Blind we seem to she who knows of fate
Our perfect gift will be lost, unbidden

In death

Learn how the knife follows your hand
One demand
Held tight the tool that feeds you
Service of my work showed her
How my tastes would kill me

Little else was so absurd to her
Mortal palate
Than the sordid flavor of being I provided
The privilege of my hunger for the end
Yet, we will dine together

What of Words

What of words
Of my words
The thoughts scribbled in my mind
How many have gone unwritten

How am I to use these words
Thoughts I have of thoughts
I've forgotten so many
Were they spelled right

Who can I trust to read
My story finished
Those unlikely pages
Illuminated by my fear

What of my words
Weightless between us
As they float away
How else am I to show you

Those words —they are me

Don't Die

No question lingers quite as long
Minutes, hours, the past reminds her
What time itself could take from her
Any and every thing and one

'Goodbye' be the gift of few
Those who find by way of parting
Peculiar peace
How calm the field after a battle

Hopefully she thinks of safe return
And if but one amongst her lot
Delights as she in having not
A question yet for both perhaps occurs

'Will I see you again?'

No more did she defer
To mystery by asking
Clearly she is known to I
When she says "Don't die."

The Girl with Lice-colored Hair

It is by fear of loss
That love is known
Through fear of failure
Courage grown

All paths are trodden betwixt
Ways defined by what is found beside

Our many feet upon the earth thus make a
passage known

One by one, thus begun
To final destination

Oft along these shaded trails
Travelers appear
Comrades in their walks of life
By partnership avail

Common peril teaching both
What we have to share

The lessons of our hardships and how from them
we grow

Needle and Brush

He shows me his desire
A colorful bird, short of wing
It seems to fly
The artist's clever trick
Soon again will the cheerful swallow
Feel the wind
Careful hands compose its form
A new home on soft skin
All things by needle created
In time are faded
Until then, the swallow sails on human wind

Can the canvas see
Yet untouched
What it is to be
Can it feel the stroke of my brush
As I layer upon it
The color of my emotions
Does the canvas know
That it is my masterpiece
Or has it been smothered
Its perfect form of infinite potential
Marred and defaced
In pursuit of my expression
Does the canvas know

Of sacrifice
For it will bear my work and name
Itself the object of my acclaim
Long after the inevitable day
I cannot wield that dangerous weapon
The brush

Don't Put Me on the Spot

For one who plays
"Plays what?"
It all, of course
For one who plays it all
Inspiration seems to come from some eternal
font

For one who plays it all
To compose is
Like taking a breath
"The mantis is the most musical insect"
He says these things

To inspire me
But if I pose to him
Such a request of my own
"Don't put me on the spot", he says
Like the humble albatross

He and his rookery
Squawking in a chorus
Cowboys and Angels
All drink from their cups
Filled by their fountain of truth

Family Business

None have shown me
Quite so well as you
What is to be done for those you love
And what visitations those who hurt them
Might have of you

Though we know each other only little
Our kin we've come to share
Family as such unknown to me before
Have to me made clear
Family Business

In dreams I've found myself beside you
Shared our fate of isolation
Yet in that place of my great fear
I was glad of that peculiar chance
To share with you our family business

What She Knows

What of her good and humble work
What of her old fears and failures
What can be said of one who has kindled fire by
conducting the business of life

She knows

What weary work makes of a woman
What in secret oft is only told
Why no more work could be done to make that
fire grow

Still she knows

By joy of love, by painful toil
For days or years, but only moments hereafter
She would come to light a fire whose warmth
she'd never feel

Perhaps she knew

Words as these would pain her to hear
As they are for me to write them
Left unknown to her, this regret
Is my love

I hope she knew

12

Destined for What?

He doesn't write — no way
An editor by something unlike trade
Limited as one can be by insecurity

For those who've seen his words
Not in text, for such is meant
Never to be seen

Instead, it must be said
Orated and demonstrated
And in that act none but he can believe

He doesn't write — certainly not

Repeated of such a pondered thing
Becomes a truth
And by such assures his destiny

He doesn't write — a tragic destiny

Intervene

Beyond, whence something always better comes
So too, and more certain, something worse
Inevitably
Our paths winding in between
How, then, are we to know that space?
What more does that emptiness need of we
Who must traverse it?

On my reciprocal shore grows a
Single shrugging flower
In whose unblinking eye does even the sun shine
Hidden
Self-evident, bound to the past
The fire from which all flames arise

I pull that flower from its earthen embrace
Below, the roots reach
Endlessly
Bound to all things
So, I pull closer Nothing and Everything
By that tender being

Distant shores joined, once more
Curvature revealed as we
Descending

Move beyond ourselves
Nothing and Everything
The Living Earth our domain

Aswirl

Oh, world! What lush and verdant form
you have, by sun's rays and river's ways
In trodden soil the living Earth birthing
The fabric of all things

A swatch of Calliopsis, cautiously petaled
The Lupine's palette painted across the evening
sky
Sweet Sorel hides beneath Hemlock's boughs
But, there, amid the sheltering fronds of Ferns

An auburn wave
Unknown to me by touch or taste
Bobbing floral heads of sunlit hue
Having once escaped my notice, grow anew

"For how in this great forest
And for how long
Have you flourished among my kin
Without me stumbling upon you?"

By impression I learn
Of peculiar places and clever forms
In which that tawny flower grows
And -- oh, world! -- where it does not,

I see those petals aswirl in the wind,
Find in dappled light the pattern of its skin
In all things, inevitably, must its presence I
observe
Lingering about me, the aroma of my desire

Effortless

By what force?

Earth in flux, inspired touch, any means as such
Peculiar ways how change occurs
As it always must
Might someday,
Whatever way, cause a stone to turn

Moved as such
Though still in place
 Might that stone in kind
Turn instead the world about itself

A new face revealed, the prior hidden
That stone is changed
By hand, by world, by all things
And all things are changed in kind

What can be asked of that stone
As it turns the world about us
As it gazes into time
What can be asked of a stone

En Passant

Morphy, Tal, Emanuel Lasker
Sat upon the board
Would the lady like to play?
My friend, you'll have to ask her

By chance or dint of circumstance
We found ourselves aface
Opponents for a single game
The victor our romance

We're pieces on the board
In life and death the lord will check
And capture with our bones

Pieces on the board
Rank and file we shout and sing
We'll meet again in passing

Capablanca, Alekhine
Make your brilliant move
By your hand we fall or stand
Our fate be your design

My piece the pawn, the king begone
War's no gentleman's sport

Would you, brother, care to pray?
My friend, we'll see the dawn.

We're pieces on the board
In life and death the lord will check
And capture with our bones

Pieces on the board
Our rank and file shout and sing
Again we'll meet in passing

Kasparov, Steinitz, Bobby Fischer
If I were home I'd kiss 'er
Entrenched alone, my wish be so
My presence carries with her

By lord's command a man is lost
His toil and strife forgone
One of us in kind will be
For victory what was tossed

Now it's done, our song unsung
The words forgotten after
That melody sticks with me
And the board remembers me when I was young

We're pieces on the board
In life and death the lord will check
And capture with our bones

Pieces on the board
Our rank and file shout and sing
Again we'll meet in passing

Behind Locked Doors

She never locks a door behind her
Each exit, every effort to escape
Evidence of one important truth
Security by lock and key was safe for only

Them

Tumblers bind unless she minds them
Loosing stubborn pins by will within
The door an open mouth which speaks of choice
Made at every threshold, she wonders who
might enter next but

Her

Thus conferred to those unheard
A chance to find one open
A door that gives someone like she
The rarest form of freedom

To Be

What's Missing

If you asked him what he's missing
He'd likely roll an eye
Both still intact
As a matter of fact
He scarcely knows he's lost a thing at all

By day he eats and loudly sleeps
Though long ago
On the road
I hope he can remember
We ran for miles and he never tired

Something I miss

By night he squeaks and loudly sleeps
I can't begrudge his age
But these days
To my dismay
The bed is higher than his desire
To climb and sleep beside me

If he knew what he was missing
Anaesthetized and bare
His happy face
And perfect gait

Concealed any ire

What's missing might only be a dog's spare leg
But soon I know
It's him that I'll
Have lost and ask "What's Missing?"

The Weight of Wings

Once again
My finger is blessed
By love's weight

You may rest your wings
My hand and heart as shelter
You might find your way

Butterfly
Metamorphosize
To flee me

-

Now your absence weighs
More than that perfect burden
I myself did claim

Dreams of nightshade offered hints
How our sun-forged pact of love might be
eclipsed
Such fragile wings spirit you away

Become something else
When as two we couldn't see

What we hoped to be

-

Darkest moon
Your bright light still shines
In the dark

Though I might yet perch
Upon some strong trusted bough
Feeling weight once held

It is you
Always felt

To Be Known by You

27

By some turn of phrase
Clever Clutch of Mumbled Words
Perhaps a sudden gasp before
Again your lips secure

A truth
Things unsaid
You wish instead
You'd left for those you love

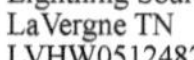
* 9 7 8 9 3 5 8 3 1 7 7 8 7 *